2010 GREATEST Pop & Rock Hits

THE BIGGEST HITS ★ THE GREATEST ARTISTS
★DELUXE ANNUAL EDITION★

CONTENTS

Song	Artist	Page
21 Guns	Green Day	2
All or Nothing	Theory of a Deadman	9
Baby	Justin Bieber featuring Ludacris	16
Beautiful World (We're All Here)	Jim Brickman and Adam Crossley	22
Cousins	Vampire Weekend	28
Crazy Love	Michael Bublé	34
East Jesus Nowhere	Green Day	54
Electric Twist	A Fine Frenzy	40
Everything to Me	Monica	50
For Your Entertainment	Adam Lambert	68
Halfway Gone	Lifehouse	63
Haven't Met You Yet	Michael Bublé	74
I Belong to You (+Mon Cœur S'Ouvre a Ta Voix)	Muse	82
Kissin U	Miranda Cosgrove	92
Life After You	Daughtry	99
Low Rising	The Swell Season	106
Need You Now	Lady Antebellum	113
Never Gonna Be Alone	Nickelback	120
No Surprise	Daughtry	126
Party in the U.S.A.	Miley Cyrus	140
Rain	Creed	133
Smile	Uncle Kracker	146
Temporary Home	Carrie Underwood	152
This Is It	Michael Jackson	158
This Too Shall Pass	OK Go	162
Undo It	Carrie Underwood	176
Uprising	Muse	168
We Are the World 25: for Haiti	Artists for Haiti	186
The Weary Kind (Theme from *Crazy Heart*)	Ryan Bingham	181
When I Look at You	Miley Cyrus	198
Who I Was Born to Be	Susan Boyle	204
Wild Horses	Susan Boyle	210

Alfred

Produced by
Alfred Music Publishing Co., Inc.
P.O. Box 10003
Van Nuys, CA 91410-0003
alfred.com

ISBN-10: 0-7390-7029-0
ISBN-13: 978-0-7390-7029-1

Printed in USA.

2010
2010

21 GUNS

Lyrics by
BILLIE JOE

Music by
GREEN DAY

Moderately slow ♩ = 84

Verses 1 & 3:

1. Do you know what's worth fight - ing for,_____ when it's not worth dy - ing for?_____ Does it take your breath_____ a - way_____ and you feel_____

3. When you're at the_____ end of the road,_____ and you lost all sense of con - trol,_____ and your thoughts have tak - en their toll,_____ when your mind_____

5. When it's time to___ live and let die,___ and you can't get an -

ALL OR NOTHING

Lyrics by
TYLER CONNOLLY

Music by
TYLER CONNOLLY, DAVID BRENNER
and DEAN BACK

*Original recording in key of Db, guitar tuned down 1/2 step.

To Coda

Verse 2:

BABY

Words and Music by
TERIUS NASH, CHRISTOPHER STEWART,
CHRISTINE FLORES, CHRISTOPHER BRIDGES
and JUSTIN BIEBER

there.__ You want my love,__ you want my heart, and we will geth - er.__ And I wan - na play it cool, but I'm los - ing you. I'll buy you

nev - er, ev - er, ev - er be a - part. Are we an
an - y - thing.__ I'll buy you an - y ring.__ And I'm in

i - tem?__ Girl, quit play - in'.__ We're
piec - es,____ ba - by, fix me. And just

Rap:
Luda!
When I was thirteen, I had my first love.
There was nobody that compared to my baby.
And nobody came between us,
Or could ever come above.
She had me going crazy,
Oh, I was starstruck.
She woke me up daily,
Don't need no Starbucks.
She made my heart pound
And skip a beat when I see her in the street,
And at school, on the playground.
But I really wanna see her on a weekend.
She knows she got me dazing,
'Cause she was so amazing.
And now, my heart is breakin',
But I just keep on sayin'…
(To Chorus:)

BEAUTIFUL WORLD

(We're All Here)

Words and Music by
ADAM CROSSLEY

Moderate pop rock ($\quad$ = 96)

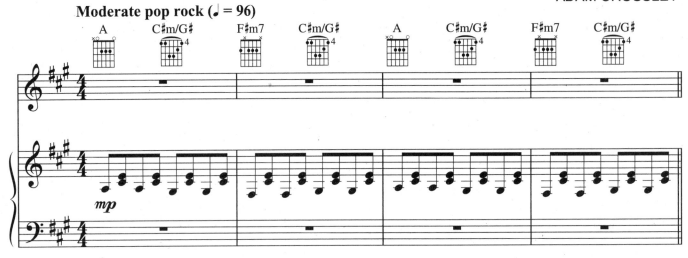

Verse 1:

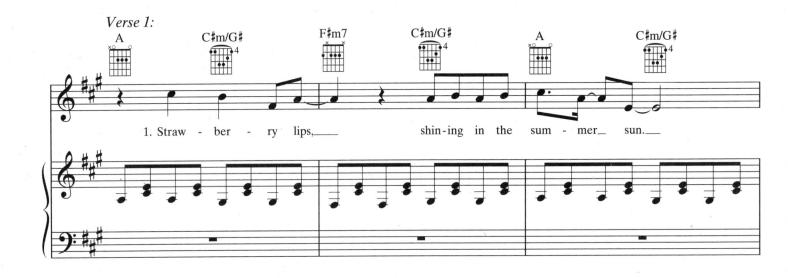

1. Straw - ber - ry lips,___ shin - ing in the sum - mer___ sun.___

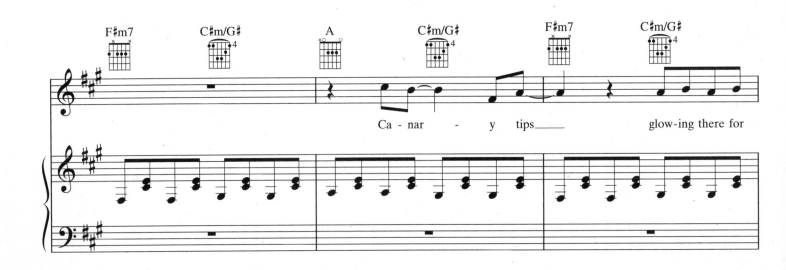

Ca - nar - y tips___ glow - ing there for

COUSINS

Lyrics by
EZRA KOENIG

Music by
CHRIS BAIO, ROSTAM BATMANGLIJ,
EZRA KOENIG and CHRISTOPHER TOMSON

*Chords are implied.

Cousins - 6 - 1

com - ing.

CRAZY LOVE

Words and Music by
VAN MORRISON

Moderately slow groove ♩ = 76

Verses 1 & 2:

Bridge:

Verse 3:

3. And when I'm re-turn-in' from so far a-way,___

she gives me some sweet lov-in',___ bright-en up my day.

Yes, it makes me righ-teous, it makes me feel whole,___

and it makes me mel-low down to my soul.___ She gives me

Chorus:

love, love, love, love, cra-zy love. She gives me love, love, love, love,

cra - zy___ love.___ (She gives me love, love, love, love,

cra - zy love._) I need a love, love, love, love, cra-zy___ love,___

cra - zy___ love,_____ cra-zy love,___ cra-zy love.___

ELECTRIC TWIST

Gtr. tuned down 1/2 step:
⑥ = E♭   ③ = G♭
⑤ = A♭   ② = B♭
④ = D♭   ① = E♭

Words and Music by
ALISON SUDOL

1. You__ should be

wild - er;   you're no___ fun at all.___

Verse 1:

Electric Twist - 10 - 10

EVERYTHING TO ME

Words and Music by
DENIECE WILLIAMS, FRITZ BASKETT,
CLARENCE McDONALD, CAINON LAMB
and MISSY ELLIOTT

Everything to Me - 4 - 1

EAST JESUS NOWHERE

Lyrics by
BILLIE JOE

Music by
GREEN DAY

East Jesus Nowhere - 9 - 1

58

ow of____ doubt. And I'll be dressed___ up in____ my___

Sun - day____ best.___ Say a prayer for the

fam - i - ly. Drop a coin for hu - man - i - ty.

Ain't this u - ni - form so flat - ter - ing? I nev - er asked you a

Chorus:

mis-sion-ar-y pol-i-ti-cians, and the cops of the new re-li-gion.

HALFWAY GONE

Words and Music by
JASON WADE, KEVIN RUDOLF,
JUDE COLE and JACOB KASHER

Halfway Gone - 5 - 1

FOR YOUR ENTERTAINMENT

Words and Music by
CLAUDE KELLY and LUKASZ GOTTWALD

*Recorded in E♭ minor.

For Your Entertainment - 6 - 1

HAVEN'T MET YOU YET

Words and Music by
MICHAEL BUBLÉ, ALAN CHANG
and AMY FOSTER

Haven't Met You Yet - 8 - 1

I BELONG TO YOU
(+ MON COEUR S'OUVRE A TA VOIX)

Words and Music by
MATTHEW BELLAMY

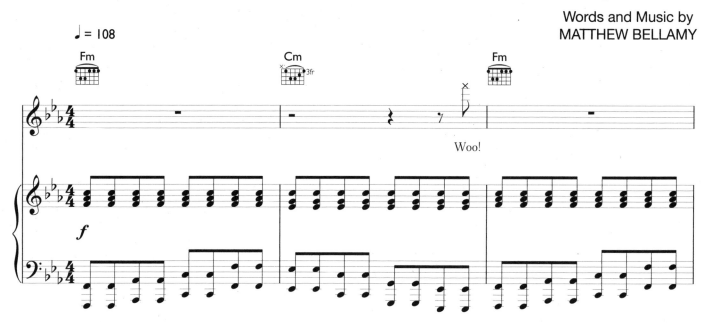

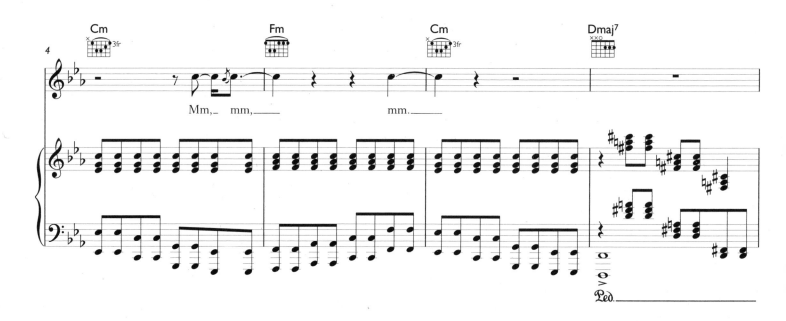

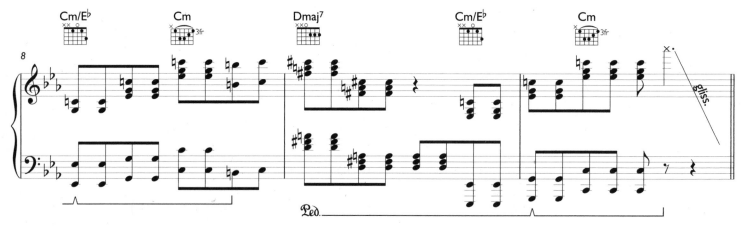

I Belong to You - 10 - 1

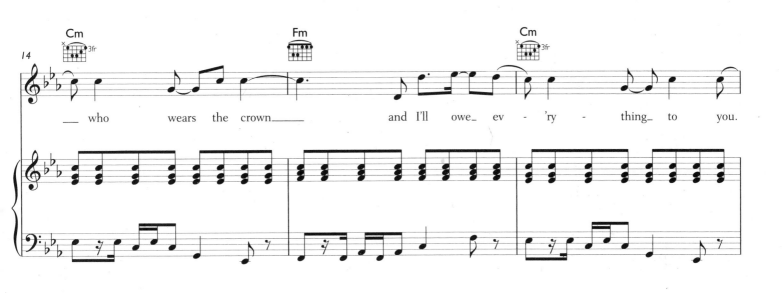

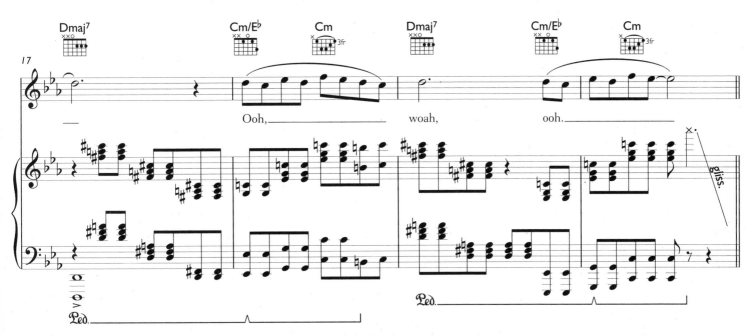

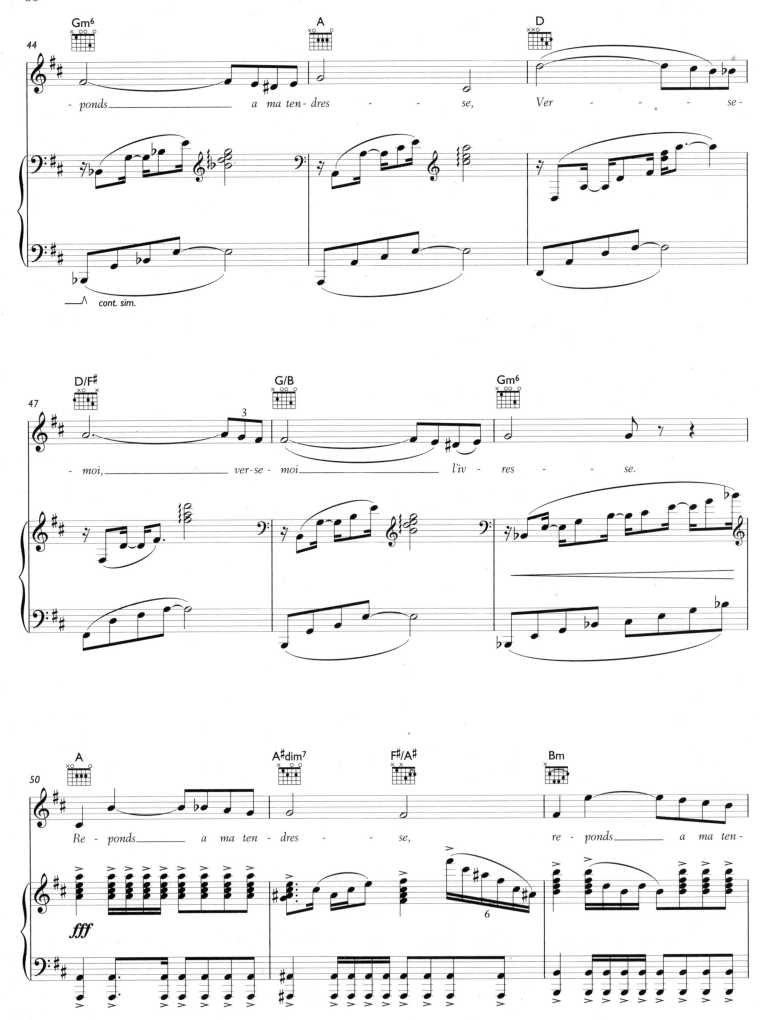

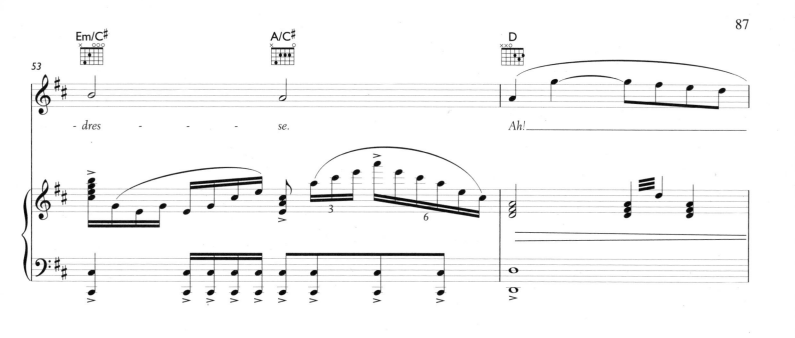

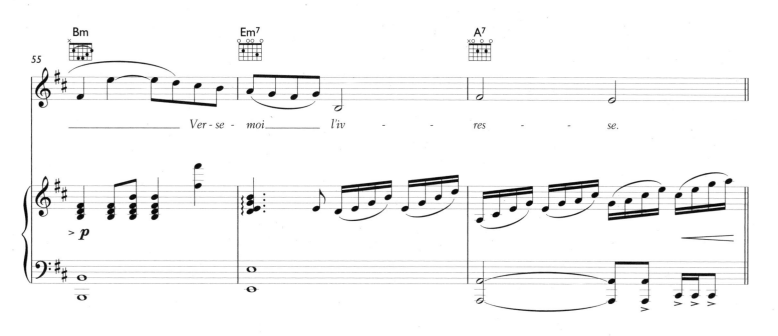

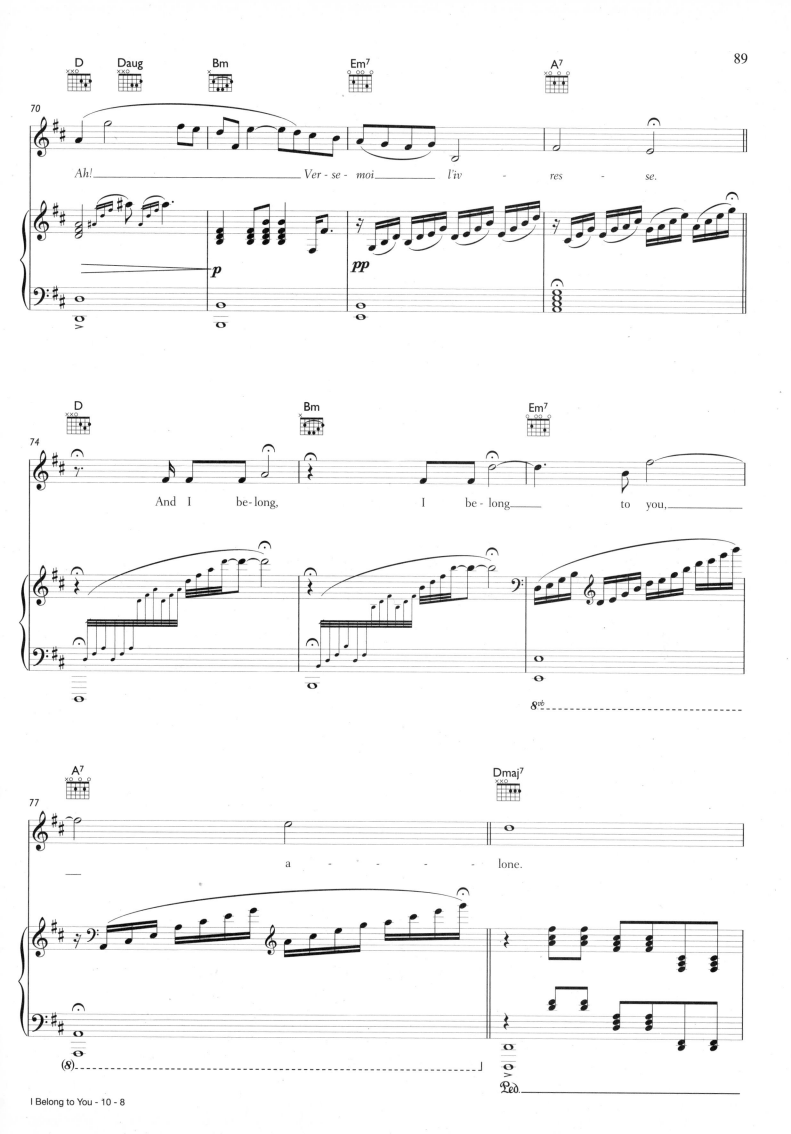

KISSIN U

Words and Music by
CLAUDE KELLY, LUKASZ GOTTWALD
and MIRANDA COSGROVE

LIFE AFTER YOU

Words and Music by
CHAD KROEGER, JOEY MOI,
BRETT JAMES and CHRIS DAUGHTRY

Life After You - 7 - 1

Freely

LOW RISING

Words and Music by
GLEN HANSARD

Slow R&B groove ♩ = 80

1. I want to sit you down and talk. I want to pull back the veils___ and find___
2. I want to take you to the rock. I want to jump right___ in___ and see

Low Rising - 7 - 1

112

NEED YOU NOW

Words and Music by
DAVE HAYWOOD, CHARLES KELLEY,
HILLARY SCOTT and JOSH KEAR

*Alternate between open G and A on the 3rd string.

Oh,__ ba - by, I need__ you now.__

Female:

NEVER GONNA BE ALONE

Moderately slow ♩ = 69

Verse:

Words and Music by
CHAD KROEGER and MUTT LANGE

NO SURPRISE

Gtr. tuned down 1/2 step:

⑥ = E♭   ③ = G♭

⑤ = A♭   ② = B♭

④ = D♭   ① = E♭

Words and Music by
CHAD KROEGER, CHRIS DAUGHTRY,
RUNE WESTBERG and ERIC DILL

And I hope.____

____ And I hope.____

Verses 1 & 2:

1. I've prac-ticed this for ho - urs, gone 'round and 'round,____ and now I
2. It came out like a riv - er once I let it out,____ when I

No Surprise - 7 - 1

Verse 3:

ing look___ that's left___ your eyes, that's why___ this comes___ as no,___

_____ as no sur - prise._____

3. If I could see the fu - ture and how this plays out, I bet it's

bet - ter than where we are now._____ But af - ter go - ing through this, it's eas - i - er to

RAIN

Words and Music by
SCOTT STAPP and MARK TREMONTI

All gtrs. in Open B5 tuning:
⑥ = B ③ = F♯
⑤ = F♯ ② = B
④ = B ① = B

Moderately ♩ = 100

Verse:

1. Can you help me out,_____ can you lend____ me a hand?__
2. I tried to fig - ure out,_____ I can't un - der - stand__

Rain - 7 - 1

Chorus:

I feel it's gon-na rain____ like this____ for days,____

____ let it rain down____ and wash____ ev-'ry-thing

____ a - way.____ I hope that to - mor - row the sun____ will shine,

I feel it's gon-na rain____ like this,____ rain____

PARTY IN THE U.S.A.

Words and Music by
CLAUDE KELLY, LUKASZ GOTTWALD
and JESSICA CORNISH

Moderately ♩ = 96

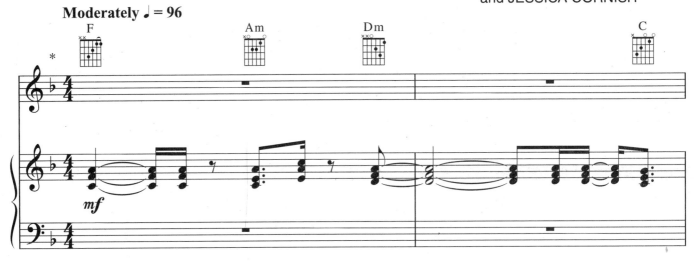

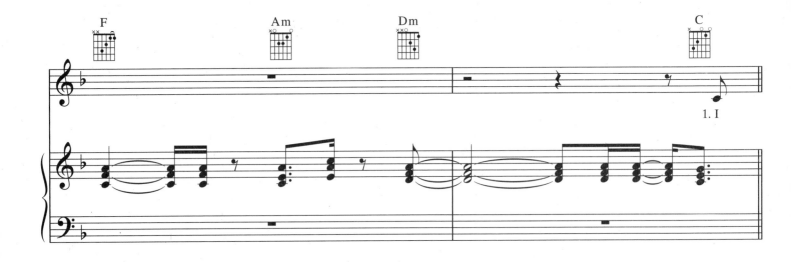

Verse:

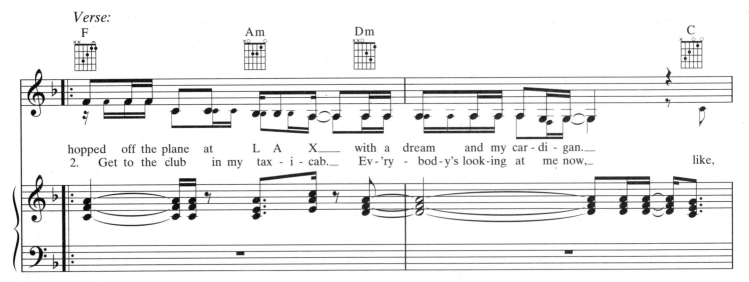

hopped off the plane at L A X___ with a dream___ and my car - di - gan.___
2. Get to the club in my tax - i - cab.__ Ev - 'ry - bod - y's look-ing at me now,___ like,

*Recording in F♯ major.

Party in the U.S.A. - 6 - 1

SMILE

Words and Music by
MATTHEW SHAFER, BLAIR DALY,
J.T. HARDING and JEREMY BOSE

Slow groove, half time feel ♩ = 72

Smile - 6 - 1

Verses 1 (cont.) & 2:

Chorus:

TEMPORARY HOME

Words and Music by
CARRIE UNDERWOOD, LUKE LAIRD
and ZAC MALOY

1. Lit-tle boy six years old, a lit-tle too used to be-ing a-lone.

2. Young mom on her own, she needs a lit-tle help, got no-where to go.

An-oth-er new mom and dad, She's look-ing for a job, look-ing for a way out.

Temporary Home - 6 - 1

Chorus:

THIS IS IT

Written and Composed by
MICHAEL JACKSON
and PAUL ANKA

THIS TOO SHALL PASS

Words and Music by
DAMIAN JOSEPH KULASH, JR. and TIMOTHY NORDWIND

Moderately slow ♩ = 80

(Ooh._____) 1. You know, you

Verse 1 (sing first time only):

can't_ keep let-tin' it get_ you down, and you can't keep drag-gin' that dead weight a-round.

Verse 2 (sing second time only):

kids_ from danc - in', why would you want_ to, es - pe-cial-ly when_ you're_ al-read-y get-tin' yours?

If there ain't all that_ much to lug a-round, bet-ter

'Cause if your mind_ don't move and your knees don't bend, well,

This Too Shall Pass - 6 - 1

run like hell__ when you__ hit the ground.__ (Ooh._____

don't go blam-in' the kids__ a-gain.

Chorus:

__) When the morn-ing comes.__   When the morn-ing comes.__

1.

2. You can't stop these __

2.

UPRISING

Words and Music by
MATTHEW BELLAMY

Uprising - 8 - 1

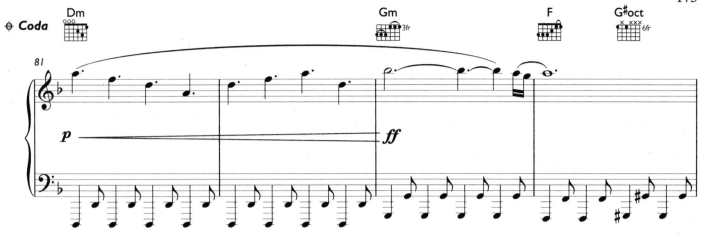

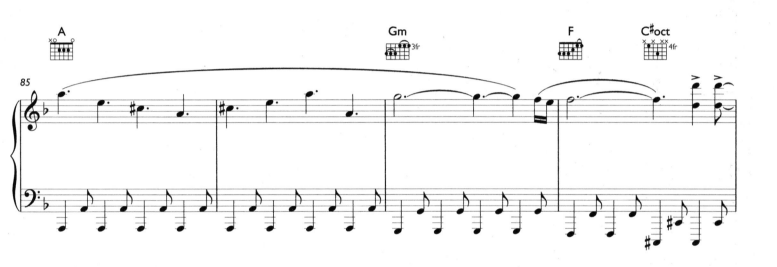

UNDO IT

Words and Music by
CARRIE UNDERWOOD, KARA DIOGUARDI,
MARTI FREDERIKSEN and LUKE LAIRD

Undo It - 5 - 1

thing got out of hand and I let it slide.____ Now I
I'm not e - ven sad._____ Now you

on - ly have my - self____ to blame for fall - ing for your stu - pid games. I
on - ly have your - self____ to blame for play - ing all those stu - pid games. You're

wish my life could be the way it was be - fore____ I saw your face.____
al - ways going to be the same. Oh no, you'll nev - er change.____

Chorus:

You stole my hap - py. You made me cry. Took the lone - ly and took me for a ride, and I

f

178

Bridge:

You want_ my fu - ture, you_ can't_ have_ it._____ (Ah.____

I'm still try - ing to e - rase you from_ my past.____) I need you gone_ so fast.__

Chorus:
N.C.

You stole my hap - py. You made me cry. Took the lone - ly and took me for a ride, and I

wan-na uh - uh - uh - uh - uh - un - do it. You had my heart, now I want it back. I'm

Undo It - 5 - 4

THE WEARY KIND

Words and Music by
RYAN BINGHAM and T-BONE BURNETT

1. Your heart's on the loose, you rolled them sev - ens with
2. Your bod - y aches, play - in' your gui - tar,
3. *See additional lyrics*

(w/ reduced bass notes 2nd and 3rd time)

The Weary Kind - 5 - 1

The Weary Kind - 5 - 2

Additional Lyrics

Verse 3:

Your lover's won't kiss,
It's too damn far from your fingertips.
You are the man that ruined her world.
Your heart's on the loose,
You rolled them sevens with nothin' lose
And this ain't no place for the weary kind.

WE ARE THE WORLD 25 FOR HAITI

Words and Music by
MICHAEL JACKSON and LIONEL RICHIE

We Are the World 25 for Haiti - 12 - 1

Verse 1:

188

We Are the World 25 for Haiti - 12 - 4

ing._____ There's a choice we're mak - ing,_____ we're

Nou se mond la,_____ ah, ah,_____

sav - ing our__ own lives.__ It's true,__ we'll make a bet - ter day, just you__ and me.__

ah,_____ just you__ and me.__

Ay - i - ti, Ay - i - ti, A - A - A - A - Ay - i - ti, Ay - i - ti, A - A - A - A - Ay - i - ti.

Rap:
We all need somebody that we can lean on,
When you wake up, look around and see that your dream's gone.
When the earth quakes, we'll help you make it through the storm,
When the floor breaks, a magic carpet to stand on.
We are the world, united by love so strong,
When the radio isn't on, you can hear the song.
A guided light on the dark road you're walking on,
A sign post to find the dreams you thought was gone.
Someone to help you move the obstacles you stumbled on,
Someone to help you rebuild after the rubble's gone.
We are the world, connected by a common bond,
Love, the whole planet singing along.
(To Chorus:)

WHEN I LOOK AT YOU

Words and Music by
HILLARY LINDSEY and JOHN SHANKS

*Original recording in F# major.

WHO I WAS BORN TO BE

Words and Music by
AUDRA MAE BUTTS, JOHAN FRANSSON,
TOBIAS LUNDGREN and MIKAEL LARSSON

Chorus:

And though I may_____ not_____ know_ the an - swers,_ I can fi - n'lly say I'm free._ And if the ques - tions_ led me here,_____ then_ I am who I was born_____ to be._

Chorus:

WILD HORSES

Words and Music by
MICK JAGGER and KEITH RICHARDS

214

Verse 3:

Db(9)   Ab(9)   Ebsus   Eb

hors - es   could-n't drag me__ a - way.__

Cm(9)   Ab(9)   Cm(9)

3. I know I've dreamed you__   a sin__ and__ a lie.

Ab(9)   Bbm(9)   Db(9)

And I have my   free - dom,__

Ab(9)   Ebsus   Eb   Cm(9)

but I don't have much time.__   Faith has been

And wild_____ hors - es

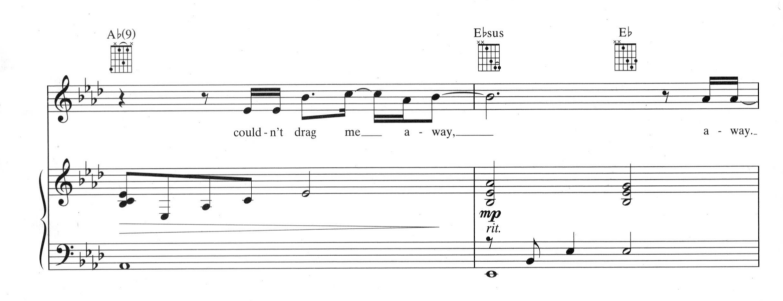

could - n't drag me____ a - way,____ a - way._

mp
rit.

Freely

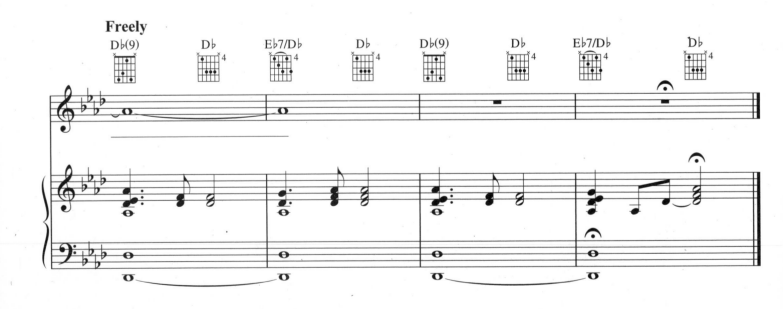